DIASPORA MISUNDERSTOOD
I Didn't Cross Oceans to Become Your Wallet
by

Thuli Marutle Leigh

Dedication

To every son and daughter who left home with
faith & fear in the same suitcase.
May you build without guilt, rise without apology,
and return whole — not drained.

Opening Quote

"We didn't leave because we didn't love home. We left so one day we can return and build it stronger."

Table of Contents

CHAPTER ONE — THE DREAM VS THE REALITY

Abroad looks glamorous until you arrive.
No shortcuts. No family to lean on.
You rebuild from zero — silently.

We don't talk enough about how heavy the first
months abroad feel.

People imagine the moment you land, the dream
begins — opportunities falling from the sky,
money growing on the pavement, life soft and
smooth because you now live "overseas." But the
truth is quieter, harsher, and lonelier.

The dream starts with struggle.

When you arrive abroad, the first thing you lose is
certainty. The second is dignity. Not because you
are weak, but because you suddenly have to learn
a new system, new accents, new rules, new
prices, new weather, new everything — and you
must do it alone.

There's no one to guide you through the job market.
No family around the corner if you run out of food.
No safety net if you fall.

Abroad humbles you in ways you never explain to anyone back home. Because even if you tried, they wouldn't understand. They see the photos — not the reality. They see the "airport glow," not the nights you question if you made a mistake.

They don't see you rehearse sentences before speaking so you don't sound "foreign." They don't see you convert every price into your home currency until it hurts. They don't see you fighting tears on public transport, pretending to be okay because you have no choice but to be okay.

This is the part of the dream no one claps for.

I arrived in London with one suitcase, two degrees, and the kind of hope that borders on desperation.
My cousin said I could stay "for a while," and I thanked God for that. I didn't have a Plan B.

He had a tiny two-bedroom flat with his wife, and the living room became my bedroom. It wasn't a bed — it was a couch that tried its best. Every morning I folded the blankets quickly so I wouldn't look like clutter. I didn't want to be a burden, even though I already felt like one.

At first, my cousin was warm, and his wife was polite.
But as the weeks went by, the air changed.

London is expensive. Food disappears faster here. Bills swallow paychecks whole. And the living room — their only place to relax — was always occupied by me. Every night I lay there pretending I didn't hear their whispers. Pretending I didn't notice the sighs. Pretending I didn't feel them wanting their space back.

Eventually, my cousin sat me down.
Not harshly. Just honestly.

He said, "You need to make a plan. I can't take care of you forever."

His words stung, but they were true.
I wasn't angry — only scared, because "making a plan" meant finding a job, and finding a job meant facing constant rejection.

I had applied for more than forty positions. I refreshed emails like my life depended on it — because it did. When nothing came through, I took the first job offered: dishwashing at a restaurant.

Night shifts.
Bleach water.
Back pain.
Hands cracking.

I used to cry on the bus home — silently.
Not because of the work, but because of the disconnect between the life I lived and the life people thought I had.

And then, my phone would ring.

Friends back home asking for money.
"Things are tough here."
"Can you send a little something?"
"You're overseas — how can you say you don't have it?"

I wanted to shout, "I'm one more bill away from being homeless!"

But instead, I said, "I'll see what I can do."

Because when you say no, you become the bad person.
Ungrateful. Changed. Selfish.
As if struggle doesn't exist in foreign countries.
As if you stop being human the moment you leave home.

Home thought I was living soft.
I was fighting to survive.

Reflection Line

Behind every airport selfie, there's sacrifice you will never see.

Chapter 2 — Beyond Airport Photos

Instagram shows the glow.
It hides the grind.

It starts with a selfie.

Passport in hand.
Smiling at the airport gate.
Caption: "A new chapter begins..."

Back home, that photo becomes proof: She made it.
What they don't see is the next photo — the one you never post.
The one where you're sitting on a bunk bed in a tiny shared flat, wondering how you'll afford the next meal.

Social media is a highlight reel.
Abroad becomes a performance.

We smile online because if we told the truth, they wouldn't believe us.
That after the airport comes loneliness.

After the glow comes confusion.
After the excitement comes exhaustion.

You learn not to post too much — not because you're hiding success, but because you're hiding the gap between perception and reality. Because the moment people see your backdrop change, they assume your bank account has too.
They think one plane ride erased your problems.
They don't know it multiplied them.

📖
Story — Dubai

When I first landed in Dubai, I thought I had stepped into a movie.

The skyline, the lights, the perfect glass buildings — everything looked so clean, so polished, so promising. I took photos on my first day, just like everyone else. Smiled wide. Posted one by the fountain outside Dubai Mall.
"New beginnings," the caption read.

What I didn't post was the flat I was sleeping in — a cramped two-bedroom apartment shared by five people. The kitchen barely fit two at once. The bathroom had a broken light. The fridge had only rice and milk most days.

I had studied tourism back home. I imagined myself working at a front desk, wearing a suit, greeting international guests with ease. But the first job I found was housekeeping. Not glamorous. Not what I had trained for.
But I took it — because reality doesn't ask if your dreams are ready.

Long hours. Heavy lifting. Quiet shifts. Some guests ignored us completely.
Others looked at us like we didn't exist.

After work, I'd go home and scroll through messages from friends asking, "How's Dubai? Must be nice!"
I'd just reply: "It's good."

Every now and then, I'd take another nice photo. Maybe in front of a luxury car. Or a hotel I didn't stay in. I knew how it looked — and that's what people wanted.
They didn't want to know about the triple shifts.
Or the stomach cramps from skipped meals.
Or the days when your body aches but you smile anyway because at least you're not back home.

I remember one time, a close friend sent me a voice note complaining about how hard life was at home. She ended it with, "At least you're lucky — you're abroad."
I wanted to reply and tell her I had 13 dirhams left to my name that week.
But I didn't. I just said, "Stay strong."

Because when you start correcting people's assumptions, they either don't believe you — or worse, they think you're ungrateful.

📖 Another Experience — Shared by a Friend Abroad

"I bought a phone with my hard-earned money, but I can't even enjoy it.
Every time I post something, my inbox fills with guilt.
Messages from home talking about how bad things are, asking for help.
I can't scroll peacefully. I can't even celebrate a small win.
Sometimes it feels like I'm not allowed to be happy."

🌱 Reflection Line

Don't let social media fool you. A passport doesn't erase struggle.

CHAPTER THREE — BLACK TAX ABROAD

Helping family is love —
but when help turns into demand,
love becomes debt.

Nobody tells you that when you leave home, you don't just carry your own dreams — you carry everyone else's too.

The moment you say, "I got a job abroad," you become a symbol of hope.
A walking promise.
A wallet with a heartbeat.

Helping immediate family is normal. It's cultural. It's love.
But the pressure doesn't stop with them — it stretches to extended family, distant relatives, and even friends who suddenly count you as their "last hope."

At first, it's small:
"Can you help with groceries?"
Then it grows:
"School fees."
"Rent."
"Emergencies."
And eventually:
"You're overseas. You can't say you don't have it."

No one asks how you're doing.
No one sees that sometimes you're sending
money you don't even have.
No one considers that you have your own
responsibilities — your own home, your own wife,
your own children who must come first.

Story — China

When I moved to China, I was proud to finally be earning something stable. I wanted to help my family and friends, not because I was rich, but because I understood struggle.

But over time, the requests became heavy.

It wasn't just immediate family anymore.
Cousins I hadn't spoken to in years started reaching out.
Friends who never checked on me unless it was payday.
People who only saw the word "overseas," not the sacrifices behind it.

One of my cousins sent me an invitation to his wedding. I congratulated him genuinely. Marriage is a beautiful thing — a blessing. But then he followed up with,
"Can you contribute? Weddings are expensive."

As if I was the one who chose a wife for him.
As if I told him to get married.
As if I'm the reason he decided to start a family.

And to think — when I got married, I didn't ask a single soul for help.
I took responsibility for my choice because marriage is not a community project; it is a personal decision. Yet here I was, being asked to help finance a celebration I wasn't even attending.

People never stop to consider that I am a family man too.
That I have a wife who depends on me.
Children who look up to me.
Bills that don't pay themselves.
Responsibilities that come before anyone else.

But to them, I'm "the one abroad,"
which automatically means I have endless money — even when I'm budgeting for survival.

And the moment you say "I can't," the guilt messages begin:
"You've changed."
"You don't care about us anymore."
"You forgot your roots."

They don't know that some months, I sent money even when I didn't know how I would eat the next week.
They don't know how many nights I stayed awake doing calculations.
They don't know how many times I broke myself to fix other people's problems.

They see the country you live in — not the life you actually live.

Love doesn't mean bleeding for everyone else.
Love doesn't mean abandoning your own family to serve another.
Love doesn't mean destroying yourself to save others.

There is generosity.
And then there is self-sacrifice.
Abroad teaches you the difference quicker than anything else.

🌱 Reflection Line

Love doesn't mean bleeding for everyone else.

CHAPTER FOUR — THE PRESSURE TO PROVIDE

"Send money."
"School fees."
"You're overseas."
As if money grows in airports.

It doesn't matter where you are — as long as you're "abroad," you're expected to provide. No questions asked.

You could be cleaning floors, sharing a room with strangers, surviving off instant noodles — it makes no difference. People back home hear one thing:
"You're earning in dollars."

To them, that means abundance.
To you, it means a salary that arrives late, gets cut, or disappears as quickly as it lands.

The pressure isn't always loud. Sometimes it's
quiet — disguised as guilt:
"It's just a little help."
"You know how hard it is here."
"You're the only one who can help us now."

Other times, it's bold:
"You have to send."
"You live overseas — you can't say no."
"Are you not ashamed to let us suffer while you're
living comfortably?"

The words differ,
but the message is the same:
Your value equals how much you can give.

📖 Story — United States

When I first arrived in the US, I worked two jobs
just to survive.
Factory during the day.
Office cleaning at night.
Four hours of sleep on a good day.

My body was always tired — heavy, slow, aching —
but my mind was worse.
I lived in constant fear of missing a shift, losing a
job, falling behind on rent. Yet every time I picked
up my phone, there was another request:
"Can you send something?"
"Fees are due."
"There's an emergency."

No one asked if I had eaten.
No one asked if I was okay.
No one asked what I needed.

But I kept sending.
Not just to friends.
Not just to extended family.
But to my younger brother — the one I trusted the
most.

I had a dream:
To build a house back home.
A place for my wife, my children, and myself.
A place where I would never again have to pay
rent or worry about being homeless.

So every month — month after month — I sent
almost everything I earned.
Telling myself, "It's worth it. When I go home, I'll
have something to show for all this suffering."

My brother assured me the building was
progressing.
He sent messages like,
"Don't worry, I'm supervising everything."
"We're almost done with the next phase."
"I'll send pictures soon."

And I believed him.
Because trust is easy when it's family.

One day, I decided to go home — unannounced.
A surprise visit.
A moment I imagined would be the happiest of
my life.
I pictured myself standing in front of my new
house, exhausted but proud.

But when I arrived, there was nothing.
No foundation.
No materials.
No workers.
No sign anything had ever been started.

My heart stopped.
My mind went blank.
All those months of sacrifice.
All the meals I skipped.
All the sleep I lost.
All the double shifts.
All the pain.

Gone.

My brother had spent everything.
Every cent I had broken my back to earn.
And he didn't even look ashamed.
He acted confused, defensive, and somehow
offended that I had come without warning.

Standing there, staring at an empty piece of land,
something inside me cracked.
Not just disappointment — something deeper.
A wound that didn't bleed, but it changed me
forever.

I flew back to the US with a different heart.
A colder one.
A guarded one.

And on that flight, I made a decision quietly,
firmly, painfully:
I am never going back home again.
Not because I don't love home —
but because home didn't love me back.

🌱 Reflection Line

You don't owe poverty as proof of loyalty.

CHAPTER FIVE — SURVIVAL JOBS

Cleaning. Factories. Night shifts.
Before success, there's humility.

They ask, "What do you do over there?"
And you pause — not because you don't want to
answer, but because you already know what they
expect.
They want success. They want glamour. They want
proof that leaving home was worth it.

To them, going abroad equals instant money.
It doesn't matter what job you're doing.
You're "earning in dollars," and that's all they hear.
So, of course, you must be rich.

What they don't see is the struggle between
paychecks.
The survival jobs.
The rent you split.
The side hustles you run after working 12-hour
shifts.
The sacrifices you make silently, while still trying
to help others who think you have more than
enough.

This belief — that going abroad means overflowing wealth — is dangerous.
It creates expectations where there should be empathy.
It turns love into leverage.
It makes people believe they can take without guilt — because "you'll be fine, you're overseas."

And sometimes, that entitlement hides in places you never expect it —
Even in the hands of the person you love the most.

Story — Canada

When I arrived in Canada, I left behind more than a country — I left my high school sweetheart.
We had dreams together.
Plans.
A future we both believed in with our whole hearts.

I promised her I would go abroad, work hard, and come back for her.
She promised she would wait.

So I worked whatever job I could find.

Cleaning offices at night.
Restocking shelves in the early mornings.
Packing boxes in warehouses until my hands blistered.

Canada didn't care about my qualifications.
It didn't care that I was educated.
It didn't care that I had potential.
It cared that I was willing to work — cheaply.

Still, every month, I sent half my salary home.
Every. Single. Month.
Even when I was barely surviving.

I paid for her university fees because I wanted her
to have a better life.
I paid for groceries for her family when they
needed help.
I even sent my bride price, and my family visited
hers.
We got married in absentia, because in our
culture, distance doesn't break commitment.

I told her, "Hold on. I'm coming back for you.
When you graduate, I will fetch you."
I worked double shifts, saved everything I could,
and counted down the days until we could finally
live the life we dreamed of.

I didn't go out.
I didn't enjoy myself.
I didn't waste a cent.
Because my goal was simple:
Build a future for the woman I loved.

Even flight tickets were expensive.
So I told her to be patient, that once I was stable,
I would fly home and come for her properly.

I thought loyalty was enough.
I thought love would protect us.
I thought sacrifice meant something.

One day, after years of grinding and saving, I saved enough for a ticket and decided to go home — unannounced — to surprise her.
To see her smile.
To watch her graduate.
To finally begin our life together.

But when I got home, the surprise was mine.

She had given birth.
To another man's child.
And she was living with him — comfortably.

Both of them had been living off my hard-earned money.
Every cent I sent with love, trust, and sacrifice...
was feeding another man and building another home.

I stood there, looking at the life I thought I was building, only to realize the foundation was gone. My heart didn't just break — it collapsed.

I flew back to Canada a different man.
Colder.
Quieter.
Wiser.

I learned that sometimes, the person you sacrifice everything for...
never deserved you in the first place.

🌱 Reflection Line

There is dignity in starting again — even when you must rebuild yourself too.

CHAPTER SIX — LONELINESS & MENTAL HEALTH

Homesickness hits harder than cold winters.
You smile outside, cry inside.

No one talks about the silence.

We speak about money, work, success, and visas
— but not about the long nights. Not about waking
up in a room where no one says your name with
love. Not about eating meals in silence,
surrounded by people, yet feeling completely
alone.

Loneliness abroad is different.
It's not just distance — it's disconnection.
You're in a new place, with no one who knows you.
No familiar voices. No family footsteps. No
random visits. No shared history.

Just time zones.
Weather you're not used to.
And a phone that rings only when someone needs
something.

Some days, you'll go hours — even days — without speaking to anyone.
You'll feel invisible.
And then your phone lights up — not with "how are you?" but "can you send?"

Mental health is hard to talk about in our communities.
You're expected to be strong.
You're abroad — you're supposed to be grateful.

But no one tells you that depression doesn't care about geography.
That panic attacks can follow you across oceans.
That even when you're surrounded by skyscrapers, you can still feel like you're drowning.

And what makes it worse?
You can't explain it to the people back home.
Because they'll say: "You're suffering where people want to go?"
As if location cancels emotion.
As if living abroad means you've lost the right to struggle.

What We Wish You Knew

(Letter to Home)

Dear Family,

I know you miss me.
I know you worry.
I know life hasn't been easy for any of us.

But sometimes, when my phone lights up with
messages asking for help, it drains me — because
I've already given everything I have that month.

I wish someone would just ask,
"How are you doing?"
Not "Can you send?"

Ask if I'm eating well.
Ask if I've slept.
Ask if I made it to work on time today.
Ask if I cried in the shower again last night.
Ask if I feel safe, if I feel seen, if I feel like myself
anymore.

Not because I want pity.
But because I miss being asked how I'm doing
before being asked for something.

I'm not your emergency fund.
I'm your child.
Your sibling.
Your friend.

Please — check on me like I matter, even when I
have nothing to give you.

With love,
Me — still trying, still carrying it all

What We Wish You Knew (Time Zones)

Please stop calling at 3AM.
I know you don't mean harm.
I know it's daytime for you.
But over here, I haven't slept. I have work in a few hours. I'm exhausted.

It's not just about the time —
It's about respect.

I don't want to wake up to five missed calls, three voice notes, and two messages asking why I'm ignoring you.
I'm not ignoring you —
I'm just trying to survive a full day on four hours of sleep.

Please understand —
I'm in a different country, a different life, a different kind of pressure.
Time zones exist, and so do boundaries.

Respect my rest.
Respect my space.
Respect my humanity.

Because love without respect is not love at all.

🌱 Reflection Line

You are allowed to be soft — even when you've
been strong for too long.

CHAPTER SEVEN — GROWTH & BOUNDARIES

Distance grows clarity.
Boundaries aren't disrespect — they're survival.

One of the most painful things about moving away is realizing how much of your "obligation" was never really love — it was guilt.

Abroad gives you space.
And with space comes truth.

You begin to see who genuinely cares for you and who only cares for what you can do for them.
Who calls to check on your heart — and who calls to check on your pockets.
You learn very quickly who misses you, and who misses the money you provide.

You start noticing patterns —
Some people only say "I miss you" when it's the 25th of the month.
Some people only call when they hear you've changed jobs.
Some people suddenly remember you exist when school fees are due.

And yet, when you say "I can't"...
you become the villain.

The Hidden Reality Abroad

People back home don't realize that many in the diaspora are not living dream lives —
some are living in the shadows of the system.

There are people working abroad without proper documents, terrified every day that a knock on the door could end everything.
People who can't go to the hospital.
People who can't complain when they're mistreated at work.
People who can't even take a proper day off because being "seen" could mean being deported.

These are the same people who send money home faithfully.

They work multiple jobs, long hours, for little pay.
They hide from authorities.
They live in constant fear.
They sleep with anxiety beside them every night.

And still —
they send money.

Why?
Because they're holding on to the hope that if
they're ever sent back home,
they will return to a house,
or land,
or savings,
or something to show for all the suffering.

But the cruel truth?

Sometimes the people back home hope they
never return,
because as long as they stay away,
the money keeps coming.

This is how some diaspora people lose themselves.
This is how pressure turns into breakdowns.
This is how kind-hearted people become addicted to alcohol or drugs to numb the pain.
This is how depression grows silently.
This is how some end up taking their own lives.

So when you see a foreigner —
be kind.
You have no idea what they are carrying.

Story — South Africa

When I first started saying no, people told me I had changed.

They were right — I had.

I had stopped overextending myself.
I had stopped sending money I didn't have.
I had stopped being available for everyone else while falling apart inside.
I started choosing peace over pressure — and to them, that looked like betrayal.

But I wasn't turning my back on anyone.
I was just turning toward myself.

There was a time when I believed that being good meant being available, agreeable, selfless — even if it destroyed me.
Now, I know better.

Some of the same people who benefited from my silence were the first to judge me when I finally set boundaries.

They didn't understand that I was fighting battles
they couldn't see —
battles with loneliness, paperwork, mental
exhaustion, fear, and responsibility.

They said, "You've changed."
They were right.
I didn't change — I healed.

What I Wish They Knew

- I'm not avoiding you — I'm surviving.
- I don't always have it.
- "No" does not mean I don't love you.
- I have responsibilities too.
- I'm allowed to rest.
- I'm allowed to choose myself.
- I still care — even when I can't carry everyone anymore.

🌱 Reflection Line

You're allowed to change without apologizing for it.

CHAPTER EIGHT — LOVE & RELATIONSHIPS ABROAD

Love abroad requires maturity — not fantasy.

People think relationships abroad are glamorous — a "power couple" building a better life.
But love abroad is not filtered.
It's pressure.
It's culture clashes.
It's stress.
And often — it's family and friends back home making things worse.

The biggest threat to relationships abroad isn't always cheating or distance.
It's the unrealistic, selfish expectations from people who expect you to keep giving — no matter what it costs your home.

You could be struggling to eat.
You could be behind on rent.
You could be deep in depression.
They don't care.
They want the money.

And when you stop sending, when you say "I can't right now,"
they look for someone to blame.

And who do they blame?

Your partner.

They say things like:

"Ever since he got married, he changed."
"That woman controls him now."
"His wife doesn't let him help us anymore."

But what they don't say is:
She's the one who kept us afloat.
She was working when I lost my job.
She fed the kids.
She paid the rent.
She helped me survive my lowest moments — and still stayed.

Story — Europe

When I lost my job, I couldn't even tell my family.
They wouldn't understand.
They'd still ask for help.
And I had nothing to give.

My wife — who is from this country — stepped in
without hesitation.
She started working extra shifts.
Covered everything quietly.
Even gave me money to send back home — so I
wouldn't look like a failure.

Can you imagine?
Taking money from your wife...
To send to people back home...
While you can't even take care of your own home?

And they knew.
Or at least they should have.
It was obvious — I wasn't working, she was.
She's from here, her family helped us when things
were tight.
The signs were clear.
But they didn't care.
Because as long as they got what they wanted,
nothing else mattered.

Some grown men back home would even say:

"Just ask your wife."
"She has money, you're abroad."
"Come on, man, she must understand."

Ask my wife?
To give money to grown people who know I'm not working?
To give up her peace for people who blame her?

This is how homes abroad fall apart.

Because every request from back home becomes an argument.
Every ignored message becomes guilt.
Every financial discussion becomes a battle.

She was carrying us.
And still, they made her the problem.

They saw her as the one blocking their access —
not the one saving my dignity.

The truth is:

Pressure from back home ruins relationships abroad.
Some marriages break not because the couple didn't love each other — but because outsiders kept taking more than they gave.

And the most painful part?
When the relationship falls apart, the same people who caused the damage will say:

"He couldn't keep a home."
"She wasn't supportive."
But they'll never admit:
"We drained them."

🌱 Reflection Line

If you care about someone abroad, protect their home — don't pressure it until it breaks.

CHAPTER NINE — COMING HOME WHOLE

I return when I am ready — not commanded.
I am building, not abandoning.

There is a strange pressure placed on people
abroad:
the expectation to return home whenever
someone calls.

It doesn't matter if you're still struggling.
Doesn't matter if you're undocumented.
Doesn't matter if you're exhausted, broke, or
fighting for your survival.
People back home will say:
"Just come."
As if life abroad obeys their timeline.

But coming home is not always simple.
For some, it's not even possible.

Some people are undocumented.
Living in the shadows.
One wrong move away from deportation.
They can't go home — not because they don't
want to — but because going back means losing
everything they've sacrificed for.

Others are working multiple jobs with no leave
days, risking everything just to stay afloat.
And some...
some never return at all.

The Harsh Truth About Diaspora Life

People back home imagine us living soft lives.
Driving nice cars.
Eating good food.
Taking pictures near beautiful buildings.

They don't see the fear.
The discrimination.
The xenophobia.
The attacks.
The stress so heavy it makes the body sick.

They don't know some people die abroad — not
because they didn't want to come home, but
because depression, pressure, or danger
swallowed them.

They don't know some return home in coffins.
Some return missing limbs.
Some never return at all.

A Real Story — And a Reminder to Be Kind

A friend of mine went abroad seeking peace — but stress pushed him into dark corners of his mind. One night, after trying to clear his head at a pub, he saw two local men beating up a third man.
He intervened.
He stopped a murder.
He did the right thing.

But to them — he was a foreigner who didn't know his place.

When he left the pub and walked home, thinking the situation was over, those men got into their jeep and followed him.

As he approached the gate of his estate, they accelerated and ran him over.

Then reversed.
And ran him over again.
And again.
Until he lay there unconscious and broken.

Security saw everything.
They had already called the police.
But it was too late.

He survived —
but he lost both his legs.
He is in a wheelchair for life.
He will never walk home again.
Never return home the same.

And people back home?
They still asked for money.
Still demanded help.
Still treated him like a bank.

No one asked what he had been through.
No one asked the cost of living abroad.
No one cared about the danger he faced as a
foreigner.
About the racism.
About the xenophobia.
About the life-threatening risks.

They just wanted what he could give.

Not Everyone Comes Home Whole — Or At All

Some people break abroad.
Some lose themselves mentally.
Some drown in alcoholism or drugs because they
can't cope with the pressure.
Some collapse from stress.
Some take their own lives.

So when you see a foreigner, be kind.
You don't know their battles.
You don't know what they left behind.
You don't know what they survived today just to
wake up tomorrow.

Not every story ends with success.
Not every immigrant gets the chance to fix their
life.
Not everyone gets to return home triumphant.

Some just survive.
Some struggle quietly.
Some never make it back.

🌱 Reflection Line

Home is not a deadline — it's a destination.
And some people are fighting battles you will
never see just to make it there.

CHAPTER TEN — AFFIRMATIONS

I am not a wallet.
I am not a machine.
I am not a bad person for choosing myself.

To every son and daughter abroad — this is your reminder:
You are allowed to protect your peace.
You are allowed to grow, rest, and set boundaries.
You are allowed to breathe without guilt.

Let these affirmations carry you through the noise:

Mental Peace
• I am doing my best, and that is enough.
• I am allowed to rest.
• I do not need to explain my silence.
• I do not need to be everyone's solution.
• My emotions are valid, even when others don't understand them.
• It's not my job to suffer to prove loyalty.

Money & Boundaries
- I am not a bank.
- I am not a wallet.
- I am not a failure because I can't send money today.
- I am allowed to say no without guilt.
- Helping doesn't mean sacrificing myself.
- I am not responsible for everyone's survival.

Family, Home & Return
- I do not need to return on demand.
- I will go home when I am ready, not when pressured.
- I am building, not abandoning.
- My journey is different — and that's okay.
- I carry home in my heart, even when I'm far.

Love & Self-Worth
- I am not ungrateful — I am human.
- I am worthy of love that doesn't drain me.
- I deserve relationships that nourish me.
- I deserve kindness — from others and from myself.
- Saying "no" is not rejection — it is protection.

For the Diaspora

- I am more than what I send.
- I am not selfish for choosing myself.
- I am allowed to protect my family abroad.
- I am not a disappointment.
- I am seen.
- I am enough.

Let these words be your armor.
Let them remind you that your story matters.
Let them silence the guilt, the shame, and the
pressure.
You are not just surviving —
you are rising.

Frequently Asked Guilt-Trips — and How to Respond

Sometimes, the words sound innocent…
But underneath, they're guilt-trips disguised as love.
Here's how to recognize them — and how to respond with truth and boundaries:

1. "You forgot where you came from."
No, I didn't. That's why I'm still sending, even when I can't afford to.
I remember where I came from — but I also know where I'm going.

2. "You have it easy there."
Have you ever lived in a country where you have no family, no support, and fear losing your job every day?
It's not easier. It's just quieter — because I don't complain to you.

3. "You're the only one we can count on."
Then who do I get to count on?
I love you, but I cannot carry everyone. I need help too.

4. "So now you're too good for us?"
No — but I'm not willing to destroy myself to prove I still belong.
Growth isn't arrogance. It's survival.

5. "Just ask your partner, they must understand."
My partner is already doing more than you know. Respect my home.
It's not their responsibility — and it's not okay to make them the backup plan.

6. "God will punish people who abandon their family."
God also wants me to live in peace, not in burnout.
Saying no is not abandoning anyone. It's being honest about my limits.

7. "We raised you, and now look how you treat us."
And I've never stopped giving back. But I'm not your retirement plan.
Love without limits becomes exploitation.

8. "Why don't you just come back?"
Because coming back without peace is not a homecoming — it's a collapse.
I'll come back when I'm whole, not when guilt tells me to.

10 Lies Diaspora People Are Told — and the Truth Behind Them

1. Lie:
"You're rich now."
Truth:
I'm surviving — sometimes barely. Earning abroad doesn't mean I'm thriving.

2. Lie:
"You're living the dream."
Truth:
It's not a dream — it's daily sacrifice, loneliness, and hard choices.

3. Lie:
"You have no problems there."
Truth:
I have problems I can't even explain — and no one to lean on when they hit.

4. Lie:
"You can't say you don't have it — you live overseas!"
Truth:
Living abroad doesn't erase bills, debt, or reality.

5. Lie:
"If I were you, I'd be rich already."
Truth:
You wouldn't. You'd be doing what I'm doing — surviving.

6. Lie:
"You just don't want to help."
Truth:
I've helped more than I can afford — I just can't do it every time.

7. Lie:
"You've changed."
Truth:
Yes — because life changed me. Because survival changed me.

8. Lie:
"You think you're better than us now."
Truth:
I don't think I'm better. I just don't want to keep breaking myself to be accepted.

9. Lie:
"It's just money — you'll make more."
Truth:
It's not "just money." It's my time, my health, my sleep, my effort. Every cent has a story.

10. Lie:
"We'll be here when you return."
Truth:
Maybe. But when I needed support — most of you were only watching your phones for a transaction.

To the One Carrying It All

You are doing enough.
Your story is valid.
Your sacrifice is seen.

To every son and daughter carrying entire
households across oceans —
This book was written for you.

For the ones who wake up before sunrise and
sleep long after midnight.
For those who smile on video calls while silently
battling depression.
For the ones sending money they don't have, to
people who will never say thank you.
For those who are blamed when they say "no,"
and forgotten when they say "yes."
For the ones who left home with faith and fear in
the same suitcase —
I see you. I hear you. You matter.

This book is not an explanation.
It is a boundary.
A reminder.
A mirror.
A soft place to land when the world gets too loud.

If no one has told you lately:
You are not a disappointment.
You are not a failure.
You are not just what you give.
You are allowed to protect your peace.
You are allowed to come home when you're ready
— not when they call.

Keep building.
Keep healing.
Keep growing.
And if you choose to go back one day,
May you return whole — not drained.

About the Author

Thuli Marutle Leigh
For every dreamer building across oceans.

Thuli Marutle Leigh is a storyteller and truth-teller whose words speak directly to the heart of the diaspora experience. Her writing reflects the weight of silence, the strength in survival, and the beauty of boundaries. Born at home but called abroad by purpose, she writes not to explain herself, but to give voice to those who are too often unheard — those carrying families across borders, sending money with trembling hands, and healing quietly while the world demands more.

This book is not her first, and it won't be her last. Thuli continues to write for the misunderstood — the ones who feel guilty for growing, tired of giving, and unseen despite their sacrifices. Through her work, she reminds us: your story matters, your strength is sacred, and you are never alone.

www.ingramcontent.com/pod-product-compliance
Lightning Source LLC
Chambersburg PA
CBHW020618270326
41927CB00005B/393